M... es

Comprehension

UPPER JUNIOR

Mary Pattinson

Contents

Name ________________________________ Date ____________

Diagnostic assessment – Narrative / poetry

The best thing about the journey was not the hissing of the steam, the rattling and the shaking, but the things that they could see. On one side there was a bald hill and a derelict farm, on the other a deep, green, secret river that they never saw from the village or the road.

The train slowed down for they were ascending the hill to Castell Coch, the red castle; a mound of ancient stones and soft grass, a thousand years old, or more.

The red castle swept away and they were going down, fast, fast to the valley of the deserted watermill. The sun never shone here. The mill was old and cold, the base of its thick, grey walls, green from the river in flood. Owen remembered the sad stories that the villagers told about the mill in flood, and suddenly he found that they were in the darkness of the sooty tunnel that took them out of the valley. They emerged into a field of golden buttercups.

1 In Owen's opinion, what was the best part of the journey?

____

2 How long ago was the castle built?

____

3 What did Owen see when the train came out of the tunnel?

____

Set A pages 3 - 6

4 Why did the train slow down as it neared the castle?

____

5 Explain in your own words 'a bald hill'.

____

6 Why was the river 'secret'?

____

Set B pages 7 - 10

7 Why do you think the author chose the words: 'The red castle swept away…'? Do you think this is a good description?

____

8 Is Owen travelling in a modern train? How do you know?

____

9 What 'sad stories' do you think the villagers may have told?

____

Set C pages 11 - 14

Name ______________________ Date ____________

Sunday smells of bacon, eggs

Sunday smells of bacon, eggs
And hot, baked, lazing cars.
Monday smells of washing
And fresh air.
Tuesday smells of less activity,
Of ironing, tea and biscuits.
Wednesday smells lonely, bleak,
Stuck there – mid of the week –
Supported by a rhyme.
Thursday is sturdier,
Smells of rich beef stew
With dumplings we hope.
Friday smells of week-old bed-clothes
Weaving me into the body of the bed
In drowsing, rotting doze;
Yes, Friday smellz!
Splendid Saturday
Smells of shortbread, fairy cakes,
Sausages and onions,
Apple crumble and not-school custard.
Sunday again –
And Sunday ought to smell of church,
Dead mice and incense.
Sorry, but no.
It smells of ragged curtains
For home made camps
And battered old bikes,
And friends.

Name ______________________________ Date ______________

Sunday smells of bacon, eggs

Match the day with the smell by drawing a line from the day to the correct answer.

Monday	apple crumble
Tuesday	beef stew
Wednesday	bed clothes
Thursday	tea and biscuits
Friday	fresh air
Saturday	old bikes
Sunday	loneliness

Answer the following questions in sentences. Give reasons for your answers.

1 How many days smell of food? Which are they?

____

2 Which do you think is a) the author's favourite day?
b) her least favourite day?

a) ______________________________

b) ______________________________

3 Why does the author say that Sunday ought to smell of church?

____

4 Name two activities that take place on a Sunday.

____

5 Why do you think the cars are 'lazing' on a Sunday?

____

6 Why do you think Wednesday smells lonely and bleak?

____

7 Do you have a favourite day? Which day is it and why?

____

Name ____________________ Date ____________

The workhouse

It is Victorian England and after Jim's father dies, his family is turned out of their home by a cruel landlord. His sisters find a home but Jim and his mother end up at the workhouse. His mother dies and Jim has to learn to live with the other boys in the workhouse.

After the cold wash in the yard Jim had to help to clean it out with brooms twice as tall as he was. They had to sweep it till the ground was bare and clean, even if hundreds of leaves had fallen in the night and come drifting over the high walls. At breakfast the boys queued up with their bowls in their hands for bread and tea. The bread was meant to last for every meal, but if Jim tried to save it he soon had it stolen by one of the older boys.

Sometimes Mr. Sissons read to them while they were eating, always Bible stories, and his whistly voice would glide round the echoing room over the clatter of knives and forks. Jim never listened to him. All he wanted to do was to think about his mother and Emily and Lizzie.

But every now and then, Mr. Sissons stopped reading and lowered his book. He stared round the room, his eyes like round, glassy balls and his fingers cracking together. Jim stopped eating, afraid that he had done something wrong. Mr. Sissons put down his book and jumped off his dais. He came gliding down the aisles between the long tables like a thin black shadow. Jim could just see him out of the corner of his eye. He daren't for the life of him look up.

The master lunged out at one of the boys at random, pulling him away from his bench by the back of his collar and sending his bowl flying and the contents spattering across the faces and clothes of the other boys.

"Misbehaving, were you?" he said, his voice as dry as a hissing swan's. "Eating like a pig? Get to the trough, animal!" And the boy crouched on his hands and knees in front of a pig's trough that was always there, and had to eat his food from that, without a fork or spoon. Sometimes there were half a dozen people troughing, usually just for Mr. Sissons' amusement.

Name ______________________ Date ______________

The workhouse

Read the passage carefully and then put the following events into the correct order.

A	Jim has to sweep the yard.	1	______
B	Mr. Sissons reads from the Bible.	2	______
C	Jim's father dies.	3	______
D	Jim stops eating his breakfast.	4	______
E	Mr. Sissons tells a boy to eat at the trough.	5	______
F	Jim is sent to the workhouse.	6	______

Answer the following questions in sentences.

1 Who do you think Lizzie and Emily are?

____

2 What work does Jim have to do in the yard?

____

3 What would happen to Jim's bread if he didn't eat it quickly?

____

4 How does the author describe a) Mr. Sissons' voice? b) Mr. Sissons' eyes?

a) ______________________________

b) ______________________________

5 Why do you think Jim daren't look up when Mr. Sissons came nearby?

____

6 What do you think is meant by:

a) at random? ______________________________

b) troughing? ______________________________

7 Do you think Mr. Sissons is a kind person? Why?

____

8 Is life in the workhouse pleasant? Why?

____

Name ______________________________ Date ______________

De-icing the pond

The first day in winter we go down
to the pond at Clissold Park, it is so sad
because none of the ducks can get their food.
But I can't help myself laughing
at the way the webbed feet skid on the ice
like drunk ducks, ducks running a high fever,

or, more like ducks doing the moonwalk.

The next day is so cold the car window is ice.
My mum gets a green bottle from her boot,
sprays it on the window till the ice melts. Magic.
She calls the special bottle de-icer.
I don't go to the pond this day.
I know it will horrify me, those hungry ducks.

The night after, I have a fantastic idea.
I wake my mum up shouting, de-icer
de-icer de-icer. She thinks I've lost
my marbles, till I let her into my mind.
In no time we're down in the dark at the park,
with two massive green bottles, size of trees.

We float over the pond with our magic bottles.
We watch the ice melt like a frown on a cross face.
We keep spraying till we hear the first duck splashing.
Then throw in our midnight bread for good measure.
After, we're so exhausted we look like
we're drunk with tiredness walking back to the car,

or, more like *we're* doing the moonwalk.

Name ______________________ Date ____________

De-icing the pond

Read the poem carefully and then answer the following questions in sentences.

1 When she goes to the pond, what does the author find: a) sad? b) to laugh at?

a) ______________________

b) ______________________

2 She thinks the ducks look as if they are doing a moonwalk. What do you think is meant by this?

____

3 Write in your own words: 'She thinks I've lost my marbles, till I let her into my mind.'

____

4 What is the fantastic idea that the author has?

____

5 Why do you think she calls the bottle 'Magic'?

____

6 Which words tell us that the author and her mother are tired after their trip to the pond?

____

7 What time is it when they feed the ducks?

____

8 The author says they 'watch the ice melt like a frown on a cross face.' Do you think this is a good description? Why?

____

9 Why do you think the word 'we're' in the last line is written in italics?

____

Name ________________________________ Date ______________

Captured!

It is vital for Mrs. Frisby to move her family of mice before the farmer ploughs the field and destroys her home. She seeks help from some super-intelligent rats at Mr. Fitzgibbon's farm. Although they agree to move her house to a safe place, they are wary of the huge farm cat who prowls the yard like a tiger. Mrs. Frisby agrees to slip into the farm kitchen and put sleeping powder in his cat food so the rats can work without fear of attack.

Where was the cat's bowl? Mrs. Frisby looked to her right as Mr. Ages had said. There it was, blue, with words inscribed around the side. Yet something was wrong. It was not two feet from the cabinet, but more like four or five. In the corner, where it should have been, rose four round wooden legs. She realised that she was looking at the bottom of a kitchen stool.

No matter, she thought. The extra distance is just a couple of feet. Mr. Ages had not mentioned a stool, but perhaps they moved it around. She crawled to her right as close to the bowl as she could get without showing herself, and tore open the package.

Just as she did this Mrs. Fitzgibbon walked over from the stove. Her hand appeared, picked up the bowl, and Mrs. Frisby heard it thump on the counter over her head. A cutting sound – a tin opener – the scrape of a spoon, and the bowl was back on the floor. The strong fishy smell of cat food. Mrs. Fitzgibbon walked away.

Now.

Mrs. Frisby moved swiftly out into the room, across the open floor, holding the powder, her eyes intent only on the bowl. She was no longer trembling. She poured in the powder, which instantly dissolved in the moist cat food. Still clutching the paper, she turned and sped towards the cabinet.

With a bang, the lights went dim. The ceiling, which had somehow become curved, was filled with little round moons. Mrs. Frisby kept running, and her face struck a cold, hard wall of metal.

A voice shouted:

"Mother! Don't let Dragon in yet. I've caught a mouse."

Billy, the young Fitzgibbon son, had been sitting on the kitchen stool, his feet up on the rung, eating berries from a colander.

Name ______________________ Date ____________

Captured!

Read the passage carefully and then answer the following questions.

1 What is the name of the farm cat?

____

2 In your own words describe the cat's bowl.

____

3 What sort of creature is Mrs. Frisby?

____

4 What sounds told Mrs. Frisby that Mrs. Fitzgibbon was getting the food ready for the cat?

____

5 Explain in your own words how Billy caught the mouse.

____

____

6 Which words in the passage mean the same as or similar to: a) important? b) melted into?

a) ______________ b) ______________

7 There is a paragraph with only one word in it. What is the word and why do you think the author has written it in this way?

____

8 Do you think Mrs. Frisby was successful in her attempt to drug the cat? Why?

____

Name ________________________ Date ____________

Dad

But he seemed to me most glorious on Saturdays, when my mother took me to watch him play rugby at Rostyn Park. We sat in the old wooden stand, that could put splinters in the backs of your legs if you squirmed about too much. All around were men in cloth caps, who took the smoking pipes from their mouths to shout hoarse encouragement as my father, splendid in blue and white hoops, tree-trunk hairy legs gleaming in the weak winter sun, pounded towards the enemy goal-line with the ball tucked under his arm. And the crowd of opponents clustering around him like flies, leaping on to his back, hanging on there two or three at a time, 'til they fell off again and lay glaring, while my father pounded on, bent almost double.

Oh, how he could twist and turn and wriggle, 'til they finally bore him to the ground by sheer weight of numbers. And I would wait with bated breath for him to emerge from the bottom of a mountain of lesser giants. But always he rose up whole, pushing his lock of dangling hair from his eyes (he had hair in those days) or spitting blood, or even, one terrible day, a tooth. I noted carefully where that tooth fell. And, as the final whistle went, and he came off the field among his mates, steaming like a racehorse in the cold air, I crept out on to the muddy pitch, trampled by a million studded bootmarks, to search for the tooth, the part of him that was lost. I found it finally, and ran into the changing room with it, among all the muddy, naked giants, very poorly concealed inside towels, who appeared suddenly and then vanished again through the clouds of steam and the sweet smell of embrocation.

I wasn't at all afraid. I was his son.

Growing Pains

The twelfth of August.
The sun-baked ground brown concrete,
the yellow grass sparse hair
on an old woman's head,
ants like freckles

twitch between the thin wisps:
everybody lies and gasps
– except my father.

Swollen with energy he capers,
bulgy over crimson boxer shorts;
I cringe behind the apple tree –
how stupid he looks.

How childish he is:
How could he:
what if someone sees him
dressed like that –

gambolling like a loon
all flab and chest hair,
long short grey socks
and rubber flip-flops?

Name ______________________ Date ______________

Dad

Read both extracts carefully. They give very differing opinions of fathers.

Questions on the first passage:

1 a) What game is played at Rostyn Park? b) Who are the giants?

a) ______________________ b) ______________________

2 How do we know that the writer's dad is well-built and strong?

____

3 Why does the writer compare his dad to a racehorse?

____

4 Why do you think the writer wanted to find his dad's tooth?

____

Questions on the poem:

5 Describe what this dad is wearing.

____

6 What is the weather like? How do we know?

____

7 The words 'gambolling' and 'capers' have very similar meanings. What do these words mean?

____

8 Why do you think the poem is called 'Growing Pains'?

____

Question on both extracts:

9 Compare each boy's opinion of his father. Base your answer on the evidence.

____

____

Continue on the back of this sheet.

Name ________________________________ Date ______________

In the vault

John Trenchard has crept to the churchyard in the darkness of night to look for Blackbeard's treasure. He finds himself in the Mohunes vault where he stumbles upon a smugglers' cargo. When he hears the smugglers approaching he conceals himself behind one of the coffins where he stays throughout their meeting.

So the meeting broke up, and the torchlight grew dimmer, and died away as it had come, in a red flicker on the roof, and the footsteps sounded fainter as they went up the passage, until the vault was left to the dead men and me. Yet for a very long time – it seemed hours – after they all had gone I could hear a murmur of distant voices, and knew that some were talking at the end of the passage, and perhaps considering how the landslip might best be restored. So while I heard them thus conversing I dared not descend from my perch, lest someone might turn back to the vault, though I was glad enough to sit up, and ease my aching back and limbs. Yet in the awful blackness of the place even the echo of these human voices seemed a kindly and blessed thing, and a certain shrinking loneliness fell on me when they ceased at last and all was silent. Then I resolved I would be off at once, and get back to the moonlight bed that I had left hours ago, having no stomach for more treasure hunting, and being glad indeed to be still left with the treasure of life.

Thus, sitting where I was, I lit my candle once more, and then clambered across that great coffin which, for two hours or more, had been a mid-wall of partition between me and danger. But to get out of the niche was harder than to get in; for now that I had a candle to light me, I saw that the coffin, though sound enough to outer view, was wormed through and through, and little better than a rotten shell. So it was that I had some ado to get over it, not daring either to kneel upon it or to bring much weight to bear with my hand, lest it should go through. And now, having got safely across, I sat for an instant on that narrow ledge of the stone shelf which projected beyond the coffin on the vault side, and made ready to jump forward on to the floor below. And how it happened I know not, but there I lost my balance, and as I slipped the candle flew out of my grasp. Then I clutched at the coffin to save myself, but my hand went clean through it, and so I came to the ground in a cloud of dust and splinters; having only got hold of a wisp of seaweed, or a handful of those draggled funeral trappings, which were strewn about this place. The floor of the vault was sandy; and so, though I fell crookedly, I took but little harm beyond a shaking; and soon, pulling myself together, set to strike my flint and blow the match into a flame to search for the fallen candle. Yet all the time I kept in my fingers this handful of light stuff; and when the flame burnt up again I held the thing against the light, and saw it was no wisp of seaweed, but something black and wiry. For a moment I could not gather what I had hold of, but then gave a start that nearly sent the candle out, and perhaps a cry, and let it drop as if it were a red hot iron, for I knew that it was a man's beard.

Name ______________________________ Date ______________

In the vault

Read the passage carefully and then answer the following questions.

1 For how long had John been hiding in the vault?

____

2 What exactly is a 'vault'?

____

3 What did John think the smugglers were discussing as they left the vault?

____

4 What do you understand by the phrase 'having no stomach for more treasure hunting, and being glad indeed to be still left with the treasure of life'?

____

5 What evidence can you find that this story is not set in modern times?

____

6 Why did John need to 'ease my aching back and limbs'?

____

7 What do you think is meant by the phrase 'wormed through and through'?

____

8 What thoughts do you think went through John's mind while he was hiding in the vault?

____

____

Name ______________________ Date ______________

Diagnostic assessment – Letters/dialogue

Just before the start of the Second World War, thousands of children were evacuated from London and sent to the countryside to escape the bombing raids.

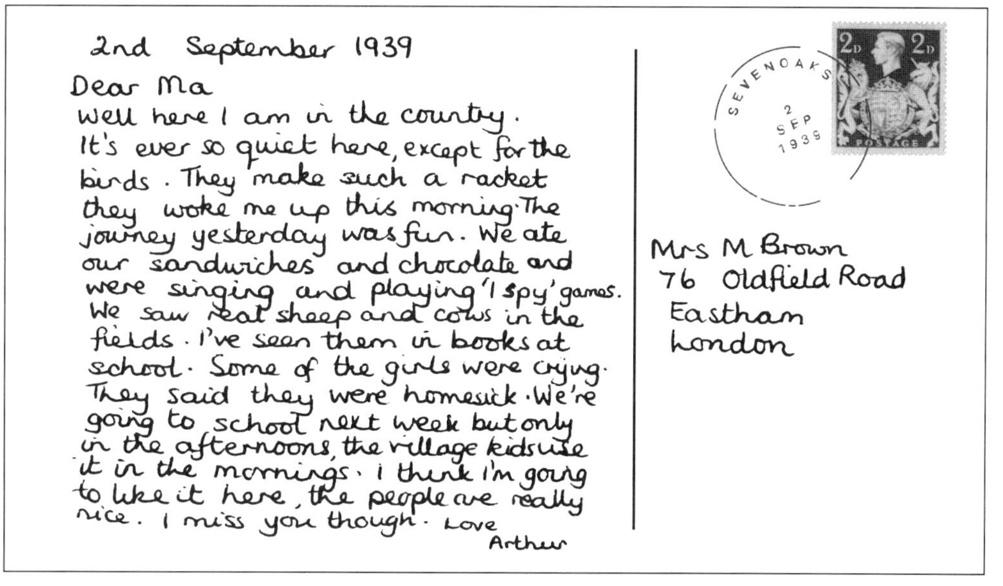

2nd September 1939

Dear Ma

Well here I am in the country. It's ever so quiet here, except for the birds. They make such a racket they woke me up this morning. The journey yesterday was fun. We ate our sandwiches and chocolate and were singing and playing 'I spy' games. We saw real sheep and cows in the fields. I've seen them in books at school. Some of the girls were crying. They said they were homesick. We're going to school next week but only in the afternoons, the village kids use it in the mornings. I think I'm going to like it here, the people are really nice. I miss you though. Love

Arthur

Mrs M Brown
76 Oldfield Road
Eastham
London

Set A pages 16 - 19

1 What is Arthur's surname? ______________________

2 What woke Arthur up? ______________________

3 Why were the girls on the train crying?

____

Set B pages 20 - 23

4 In what month did Arthur travel to the country?

____

5 Did Arthur enjoy his journey? Give reasons for your answer.

____

6 What is meant by a racket? ______________________

Set C pages 24 - 27

7 Do you think Arthur had seen sheep and cows before?
Give reasons for your answer.

____

8 Why do you think the school has to be shared?

____

9 What would Arthur have found different about the country?

____

Name ______________________ Date ____________

Sophie's party

3 Oxleys Close
Hawnes
Mon 28th June

Dear Christie

Please will you come to my birthday party? It's on Sat 3rd July. If you can be at my house at 3.00p.m we will go swimming at the Oasis Beach Pool and then come home for tea. We're going to have a sleep over so bring a sleeping bag and any good music tapes for us to listen to. Dad said he'd get us a really scary video to watch so I hope we don't have nightmares! Ask your parents if they can pick you up between 10.00 and 11.00 the next morning. I do hope you can come. It will be great fun.

Love Sophie.

14, Caves Road
Hawnes
Tues 29th June

Dear Sophie,

Thank you for your party invitation. I'm sorry but I won't be able to come. I'm really fed up about it, but Mum says we've got to visit my grandma at the weekend.

She's been in hospital with pneumonia. She's home now but isn't able to do very much so we're doing some shopping and cleaning and gardening for her. I am glad she's getting better but I'd much rather come to your party.

I'll bring your present round to your house before I go. You'll be able to listen to it at your party. (That's a big clue to what I've got for you!)

Have a great time

Love Christie

Name ______________________ Date ____________

Sophie's party

Read carefully Sophie's letter and Christie's reply. Now answer the following questions.

1 a) When is Sophie's party going to be held? ______________________

b) At what time would she like people to arrive? ______________________

c) What time does she suggest parents collect their children?

____

2 a) Name some items that Sophie's friends would *need* to bring to her party?

____

b) What else would Sophie *like* them to bring?

____

3 Why can't Christie come to Sophie's party?

____

4 What illness does Christie's grandmother have? Is she fully recovered?

____

5 What present do you think Christie will be giving to Sophie? What evidence can you find to support your answer?

____

6 Which of the following words best describe Christie's feelings about missing the party? Underline the most appropriate.

a) angry b) disappointed c) astounded d) furious

7 Do you think Sophie's friends will have a good night's sleep? Give reasons for your answer.

____

8 Would you like to go to Sophie's party? Give your reasons.

____

Name ______________________________ Date ______________

The chimney sweeps

In Victorian days small children were sent up chimneys to sweep away the soot and grime. It was a dirty and dangerous job. Harry and Beth are being forced by Scragscutt to clean chimneys in a large, rich house. He pushes them up the chimney.

Maid: Are you sure they'll be all right?
Scragscutt: Course they will, ma'am.
Maid: But they've got bare feet.
Scragscutt: All the better for climbing in the darkness. Helps them to feel for the bricks.
(Meanwhile, Harry is climbing higher inside the chimney. Beth is not far behind.)
Harry: Beth, are you all right?
Beth: I think so, but it's scary.
Harry: Make sure your feet don't slip.
Beth: It's terribly dark. And horribly smelly. There's thick soot everywhere.
Harry: I'm starting to brush now. Keep your head down. Here goes!
Beth: Harry! Soot's falling all over me! I can taste it in my mouth!
Harry: Then climb up beside me. Sooner we finish the sooner we get something to eat.
Beth: We're very high up.
Harry: You still scared?
Beth: Can't stop shaking.
Harry: Hey, what's this? Twigs ... and sticks. Must be the remains of a bird's nest.
Beth: Ugh, it stinks!
Harry: Just keep on climbing. Watch you don't slip. Hey, look up there. A patch of blue ... blue sky. We're nearly at the top.
Beth: I'm sore all over. I think my feet are bleeding.
Harry: Same here. But we're almost at the top. Just one big shove ... and the brush is out of the chimney pot. We've done it! We can climb back down.
Scragscutt: You brats up there! You lazy brats! Get down here now! You've got another five chimneys to clean. Hurry up!
Beth: *More* chimneys!
Harry: 'Fraid so, sister.
Scragscutt: I warned you! I warned you to get a move on! I'll smoke you out!
Beth: What does he mean, smoke us out?
Harry: He's burning paper, starting a fire, that's what he means. Watch out, here comes the smoke. Come on, Beth, climb down as quickly as you can!

Name ______________________________ Date ______________

The chimney sweeps

Read the extract from the play very carefully and then answer the following questions.

1 What reason does Scragscutt give for Harry and Beth having bare feet?

____

2 What three things does Beth say about the chimney?

(i) ____________________ (ii) ____________________

(iii) ____________________

3 Why does Harry tell Beth to keep her head down while he is brushing?

____

4 How do the children know when they are near the top of the chimney?

____

5 Beth says, "*More* chimneys!" Why do you think the word 'more' is written in italic print?

____

6 What had been promised to the children once they had swept the chimneys?

____

7 What did Scragscutt do to speed the children up?

____

8 Why do you think small children were used to sweep chimneys in Victorian times?

____

____

Name ______________________ Date ____________

Visit to Belgrave Manor

St. Mark's School, Woodfield Road, Barford, Middlesex, TW2 5EJ

Thursday 1st October

Dear Mr. Stuart,

I am writing to say how much the children of Class 6 enjoyed our visit to Belgrave Manor on Tuesday and to thank you for helping to make the day so interesting. It was great fun to see everyone dressed up in Tudor costume.

We have read the book 'House of Destiny' in class so it was fascinating to visit the place where Joan Barnett set her story. I wonder whether Queen Elizabeth I really did hide from her enemies in the secret room at Belgrave!

We all had our favourite rooms. Some liked the kitchen, others the Great Hall, but I think I liked the Great Chamber best of all. I could easily imagine the animal skins on the walls and all the bats and birds and insects up in the roof rafters. We were told that the canopy was to prevent all the creepy crawlies from dropping on to you in the night. The bed was really small – Tudor people must have been very short. I suppose the curtains round the bed were to keep the draughts out. It was rather cold up there. The kitchen was nice and warm, though – probably too hot if you were the spit boy who had to turn the meat in front of the fire. I expect it was very smoky too with the food all cooking on the fire. It was nice and clean when we visited but in Tudor times I think it was rather dirty. We were told that old scraps of food were dropped on the floor and mingled with the rushes which were always put down. I bet there were loads of rats and mice. Ugh!

I really did enjoy my visit but I don't think I would like to live in the sixteenth century. Would you? I think it would be a bit too uncomfortable and unhygienic!

Thanks again for a super day.

Yours sincerely,

Najeeb Patel

Name ______________________ Date ____________

Visit to Belgrave Manor

Read carefully Najeeb's letter to Mr. Stuart, then answer the following questions.

1 Which class visited Belgrave Manor? Name their school.

2 What is a 'canopy'? Najeeb was told the purpose of the canopy. What was it?

3 Do you think working in the kitchen in Tudor times would have been pleasant or unpleasant? Give reasons for your answer.

4 In which century did the Tudors reign? What reasons does Najeeb give for being glad he didn't live in those times?

5 Find two adjectives that Najeeb used to describe his day.

6 What did Tudor people use instead of carpets?

7 What do you think was the purpose of the class visit to Belgrave Manor?

8 What do you think 'House of Destiny' may have been about?

Name ______________________ Date __________

Spooky Cott

A group of friends meet together to discuss plans for starting up their own village newspaper, The Gazette. *They are seeking ideas for exciting stories.*

"We need to do something a bit more excitin', like," said George impatiently. "Let's go lookin' fer badgers or even their holes. How about it? Who's fer goin'?"

"I'd like to," blurted out Willie.

They all stared at him in surprise. It was unusual for him to volunteer without persuasion.

"I'll come too," said Zach.

Carrie and Ginnie looked at each other.

"We'll come too," they sighed in a tone of resignation.

"I ent forcin' you," said George.

"I say," said Zach. "What about that mysterious place you were talking about at Aunt Nance's?"

Ginnie paled.

"Spooky Cott," she whispered.

"Couldn't we go and look at that as well?"

George and the twins gave no answer and Willie felt a cold prickle crawl up his back and into his hair.

"Oh come on," cried Zach. "It can't be that frightening, can it?"

All three of them nodded silently.

"We ent bin there fer two years now," said George.

"I say, what happened?"

"Nothin' you could exactly put yer finger on, like," said Carrie ominously. "But there was a strange eerie feeling in the air. The trees," she swallowed, "the trees, they seemed to groan and wave their arms about."

"Let's go. I mean, if we all go together we can protect each other."

"When was you thinkin'?" asked George in an unusually timid voice.

"How about tonight!" whispered Zach.

Ginnie gave a shiver.

"Or," he continued, "Hallowe'en!" and he gave a shrieking imitation of a cackling witch.

Name ______________________________ Date ______________

Spooky Cott

Read the passage carefully and then answer the following questions.

1 How many children are there in the group? Name them.

____

2 What was a) the first suggestion of somewhere exciting to go?
b) the second suggestion? Who made these suggestions?

a) ______________________________

b) ______________________________

3 How does Carrie describe Spooky Cott as being frightening? What does she mean when she says the trees seemed to 'wave their arms about'?

____

____

4 Why do you think Willie 'felt a cold prickle crawl up his back and into his hair'?

____

5 a) When was the last time the children had visited Spooky Cott?
b) Which children have been there before?

____

____

6 Why do you think Zach suggests Hallowe'en for visiting Spooky Cott?

____

7 The following words in the passage have been spelled incorrectly to show the reader how they are pronounced. Write each word as it should be spelled.

'fer' __________ 'bin' __________ 'yer' __________ 'ent' __________

8 We are told that it was <u>unusual</u> for Willie to 'volunteer without persuasion' and that George spoke in an '<u>unusually</u> timid voice'. What do you think these two characters are <u>usually</u> like?

____

____

Name ______________________________ Date ____________

Penpals

Hattie's class has been given penpals to write to. The letter Hattie received was from Jessica. She found it very dull and boring and so, when writing her reply, she decided to have some fun!

18 Bridge Street
Attleford

Dear Penpal,
I am really pleased to have a new penpal. I will tell you all about myself. I live in Attleford, which is very nice. My house is nice too. It has three bedrooms. My bedroom is purple. My curtains are purple and my quilt is purple. I like purple. Do you?

What is your house like? Do you live in a nice house? How many bedrooms do you have? Do you have a television in your room? Or a stereo? Have you got a computer? Tell me all about yourself and your new house when you write back. I can't wait to get your letter.

Your new penfriend,
Jessica

---

1 St Augustine's Road
Medthorpe

Dear Jessica
Thank you so much for your nice letter. Of course I will tell you all about myself. I am the Hon. Henrietta Annabel Austin, but my friends all call me Hattie. It can be so embarrassing and such a bore, you know, having a title.

You are probably wondering why I attend this rather dreary school. Well, the fact of the matter is, I used to go to Eaton Grange, the exclusive boarding establishment in the heart of Buckinghamshire. Unfortunately, we fell upon hard times when my father disappeared on a big game hunt in deepest, darkest Africa. Since then we have had to sell our beautiful home and all my ponies and live a rather more frugal lifestyle. I no longer have my suite of rooms but my bedroom is pleasant enough and is decorated in tasteful cream and gold.

No, I do not have a television in my room, or a stereo, or even a computer. We believe that these modern appliances detract from the worthier things in life. Instead I like to peruse our priceless collection of antique books and practise my skills on the grand piano in the drawing room.

We have great hopes that Father may return one day and restore us to our former life of comfort. In the meantime we remind ourselves of his presence by gazing at his wonderful oil painting depicting his hunting safaris.

I have no brothers and sisters and I am somewhat lonely. So, Jessica, it is a great pleasure to have such a penpal as you.

Yours most sincerely
The Hon. Henrietta Austin (Please address letters simply to H Austin)

Name ______________________ Date ____________

Penpals

Read the letters carefully and then answer the following questions.

1 What is a penpal?

____

2 Why do you think Hattie found Jessica's letter so boring?

____

3 Hattie asks Jessica to simply address her letters to H Austin.
a) What reason does Hattie give for not using her full title?

____

b) Why does she *really* not want Jessica to use the full name?

____

4 What words in Hattie's letter mean the same as:
a) read in a leisurely manner

____

b) sparing with money

____

5 What reasons does Hattie give for having to leave her expensive boarding school?

____

6 What does Hattie enjoy doing in her spare time?

____

7 How is the memory of Hattie's father kept alive?

____

8 How many questions did a) Jessica and b) Hattie ask in their respective letters?

____

9 When Hattie had to reply to Jessica's letter, she 'decided to have some fun'.
What do you think is meant by this? Do you think she did have fun?

____

Name ______________________ Date ____________

Monday morning

It's Monday morning and Tom does not want to go to school.
It occurs to him that if he is sick he can stay at home.
He searches his body for signs of illness, decides his toe
is sore and takes to groaning to wake up his cousin, Sid.

But Sid slept on unconscious.

Tom groaned louder, and fancied that he began to feel pain in the toe.

No result from Sid... Sid snored on.

Tom was aggravated. He said, "Sid, Sid!" and shook him. This course worked well, and Tom began to groan again.

"Why, what's the matter, Tom? I must call Auntie."

"No – never mind. It'll be over by and by, maybe. Don't call anybody."

"But I must! *Don't* groan so, Tom, it's awful. How long you been this way?"

"Hours. Ouch! Oh, don't stir so, Sid, you'll kill me."

"Tom, why didn't you wake me sooner? Oh Tom, *don't!* It makes my flesh crawl to hear you. Tom, what is the matter?"

"I forgive you everything, Sid. (Groan) Everything you've ever done to me. When I'm gone..."

"Oh, Tom, you ain't dying are you? Don't, Tom – oh, don't. Maybe –"

Tom was suffering in reality, now, so handsomely was his imagination working, and so his groans had gathered quite a genuine tone.

Sid flew downstairs, and said, "Oh, Aunt Polly, come! Tom's dying!"

"Dying!"

"Yes'm. Don't wait – come quick!"

"Rubbage! I don't believe it!"

But she fled upstairs, nevertheless, with Sid and Mary at her heels. And her face grew white, too, and her lip trembled. When she reached the bedside she gasped out, "You, Tom, what's the matter with you?"

"Oh, Auntie, my sore toe's mortified!"

The old lady sank down into a chair and laughed a little, then cried a little, then did both together. This restored her and she said, "Tom, what a turn you did give me. Now you shut up that nonsense and climb out of this."

The groans ceased and the pain vanished from the toe. The boy felt a little foolish, and he said, "Aunt Polly, it *seemed* mortified, and it hurt so I never minded my tooth at all."

"There, there, now, don't begin that groaning again. Open your mouth. Well – your tooth *is* loose, but you're not going to die about that. Mary, get me a silk thread, and a chunk of fire out of the kitchen."

Tom said, "Oh please, Auntie, don't pull it out. It don't hurt any more. I wish I may never stir if it does. Please don't, Auntie. I don't want to stay home from school."

Name ______________________ Date ____________

Monday morning

Read the passage carefully and then answer the following questions.

1 How are Tom and Sid related?

2 Was Tom really ill? Did Sid believe Tom was ill? Explain your answers.

3 Explain the sentence: "Tom was suffering in reality now, so handsomely was his imagination working, and so his groans had gathered quite a genuine tone."

4 What evidence can you find that Aunt Polly:
a) was at first worried about Tom?

b) realised his pretence?

5 What is the meaning of 'mortified'? In your opinion did Tom really know the meaning?

6 How do you think Aunt Polly is going to pull out Tom's tooth by using thread and some coals from the fire?

7 What do you learn from the passage about Tom's character? Think carefully about his relationships with Sid and his aunt.

8 How can you tell who is speaking when it is not stated?

Name ______________________ Date ______________

Diagnostic assessment – Instructions

MAINTAINING YOUR CYCLE
Make sure that the:

- lights and reflectors are kept clean and in good working order
- tyres are in good condition and inflated to the correct pressure
- brakes and gears are working correctly
- chain is properly adjusted and oiled
- saddle is adjusted to the right height

CLOTHING AND EQUIPMENT
Make sure that your:

- wear a cycle helmet
- wear clothes that will help you be seen

WHEN CYCLING

- keep both hands on the handlebars except when changing gear or signalling
- keep both feet on the pedals
- do not ride more than two abreast
- ride in single file on cycle tracks and lanes
- do not ride close behind another vehicle
- do not carry anything that will affect your balance or get tangled in the wheels

YOU MUST NOT CARRY A PASSENGER

1 What advice is given about the saddle?

____

2 When can you take one hand off the handlebars?

____

3 What must you not carry when cycling?

____

Set A
pages 29 - 32

4 What do you need to do to the chain to ensure it moves smoothly?

____

5 What do the following words mean? maintaining ______________

inflated ______________ adjusted ______________ abreast ______________

6 What would you suggest is appropriate clothing for cycling?

____

Set B
pages 33 - 36

7 What dangers are there if you ride too close to another vehicle?

____

8 Which of the advice is the most important and why?

____

9 Can you give any other advice?

____

Set C
pages 37 - 40

Name ______________________________ Date ____________

How to draw dragons

Dragons are legendary monsters that lurk in dungeons and caves. They can be friendly but many are dangerous. Most dragons have scaly skin, wings and evil teeth and claws. Here is a dragon to draw.

1 HEAD AND NECK

Copy the picture to draw the head, neck and bulging eye. Then add nostrils, the other eye and spines down the neck as shown.

2 BODY AND LEGS

Draw lines for the top and bottom of the body. Add the legs. Rub out the bits shown dotted above.

3 WINGS

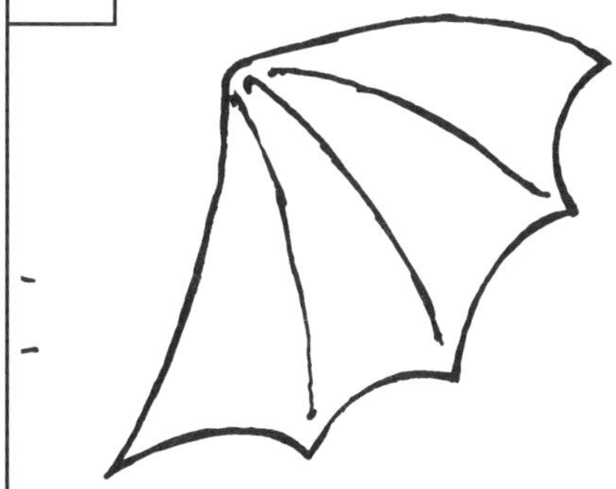

Draw a fan-shaped wing like in the picture above. It looks like a part of an umbrella with spokes going from the bottom up to the point at the top.

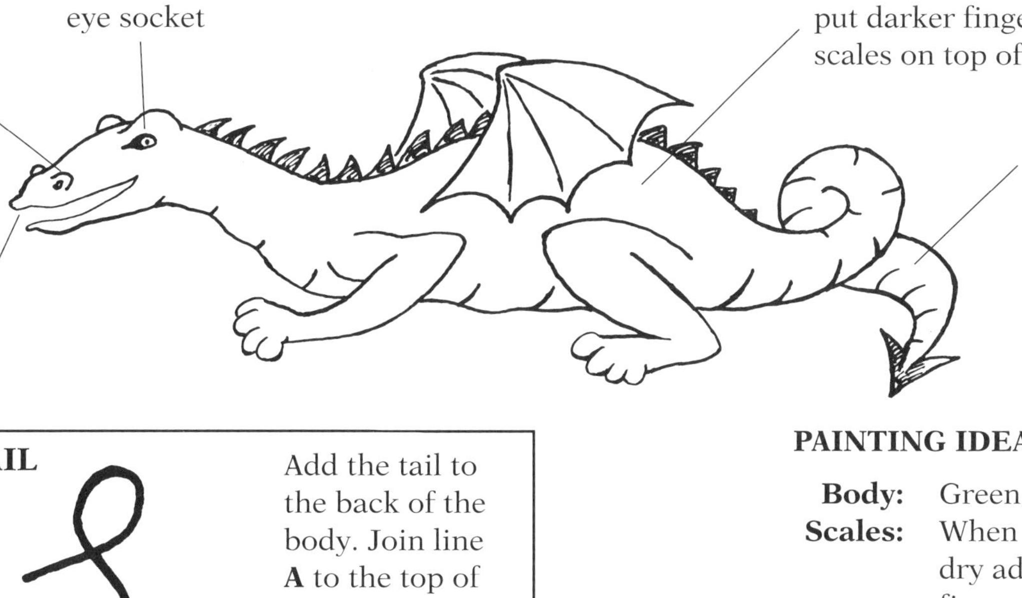

4 TAIL

Add the tail to the back of the body. Join line **A** to the top of the body and line **B** to the underneath. Rub out the dotted part.

PAINTING IDEAS

Body:	Green
Scales:	When the body is dry add darker fingerprints.
Wings:	Pale yellow-green. Do the outline and spokes dark green.
Teeth and claws:	Yellow
Mouth and eye:	Red
Nostril:	Black

Name ______________________________ Date ______________

How to draw dragons

Read the information and then answer the following questions.

1 Underline the correct answer to complete the sentence.

Dragons live in a) the sea. b) on top of mountains. c) in caves. d) in clouds.

2 Complete the sentence.

Dragons can be friendly but many are ______________________________

3 Which word describes a dragon's skin? ______________________________

4 If you are drawing a dragon, which part should you begin with?

____

5 What is a 'bulging' eye?

____

6 What shape are the wings? What do they look like?

____

7 How does the writer suggest you show the scales on the dragon's body?

____

8 What does the writer suggest that you might like to add to the dragon's head?

____

9 Some things are missing from the dragon. What are they? They would make the dragon look really fierce.

____

Add them to the drawing.

10 Colour the dragon according to the instructions.

Name ______________________ Date ______________

Butterfly cakes

Cake Mix

Required

1 egg (size 3)

30ml (2 tablespoons) of cold water

Packet of cake mix

Method

1 Preheat oven to 200°C (400°F) Gas Mark 6. Set shelf in centre of oven.

2 Place the bun cases in a tin or on a baking tray.

3 Blend 1 egg with 30ml of water in a mixing bowl.

4 Add the sponge mix and whisk with an electric mixer (medium speed) for 2 minutes. (A hand whisk may take longer.)

5 Divide the mixture equally between the bun cases. Bake immediately for 8–10 minutes until light and golden brown.

Topping Mix

Required

50g (2oz) softened butter or margarine

5ml (1 teaspoon) cold water

Packet of topping mix

Method

1 Put softened butter or margarine into a small bowl.

2 Reserve one heaped teaspoon of topping mix. Add the remaining mix to the butter or margarine together with 5ml of cold water and beat until smooth and creamy.

3 Slice the top off each cake and cut into two wings.

4 Spread an equal amount of topping on to each cake and place the wings on top. Sprinkle the butterfly cakes with the reserved mix.

Name ______________________ Date ____________

Butterfly cakes

List all the *ingredients* you will need to make these cakes.

List all the *equipment* you will need to make these cakes.

Ingredients	**Equipment**

Write your answers to these questions in sentences.

1 To what temperature should you heat the oven?

____

2 How can you tell that your cakes are properly cooked?

____

3 What do you mix with the butter or margarine to make the topping?

____

4 What does 'Reserve one heaped teaspoon of topping mix' mean?

____

5 Which word, used in both sections, means needed?

____

6 Why do you think that certain words are written in bold print?

____

7 Do you think the instructions are easy to understand for children of your age? Explain your reasons.

____

Name ______________________ Date ______________

First aid – Minor burns and scalds

Domestic accidents are the most common cause of minor burns and scalds. Prompt first aid will usually enable them to heal naturally and well, but if you are in any doubt as to the severity of the injury, seek a doctor's advice.

1 Flood the injured part with cold water for about 10 minutes to stop the burning and relieve the pain. If water is unavailable, any cold, harmless liquid, such as milk or canned drinks, will do.

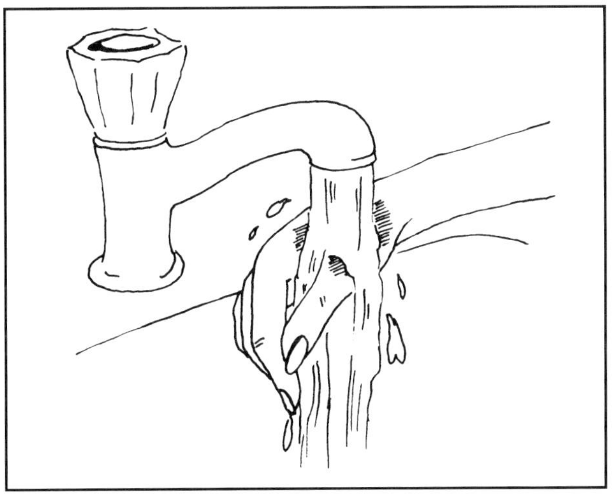

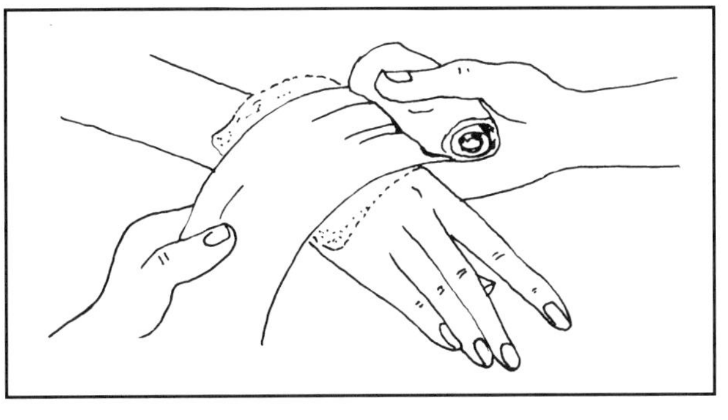

TREATMENT
Your aims are:
1 To stop the burning.
2 To relieve pain and swelling.
3 To minimise the risk of infection.

2 Gently remove any jewellery, watches or constricting clothing from the injured area before it begins to swell.

3 Cover the area with a sterile dressing, or any clean, non-fluffy material. A polythene bag or kitchen film makes a good temporary covering.

DO NOT use adhesive dressings or strappings.
DO NOT break blisters or interfere with the injured area.
DO NOT apply lotions, ointments, creams or fats to the injury.

Blisters
These are thin 'bubbles' that form on skin damaged by heat or friction. They are the result of tissue fluid leaking into the damaged area below the skin's surface. During healing, new skin forms at the base of the blister; the fluid is absorbed and the outer layer of dead skin eventually peels off.

What you can do
Never break a blister, you are likely to introduce infection.
A blister usually needs no treatment. However, if it breaks, or is likely to be damaged, cover the injured area with a dry, non-adhesive dressing that extends well beyond the blister's edges.

Name ________________________________ Date ______________

First aid – Minor burns and scalds

Underline the most appropriate answer.

1 Where do most minor burns happen?
a) at work b) at school c) at home d) on holiday

2 'Minor' means:
a) harmful b) not serious c) painful d) infectious

3 You should never burst a blister because:
a) it will be painful b) it will cause swelling c) it may cause infection
d) it will not heal

4 'Prompt' means:
a) immediate b) strict c) helpful d) careful

Answer the following questions in sentences.

5 What do you think 'minimise the risk of infection' means?

____

6 Why do you think you need to remove jewellery?

____

7 How would you describe 'constricting' clothes?

____

8 What may happen if you cover a burn with fluffy material?

____

9 Why do you think kitchen film or polythene makes a good dressing?

____

10 What treatment does a blister usually need?

____

Name ______________________ Date ____________

Party games

Winking

This is an age old favourite with both boys and girls. A circle of chairs is made facing inwards. A girl sits on each chair except one, which is left empty. Behind each chair, including the empty one, stands a boy with his hands resting on top of the chair but not touching the girl sitting in it.

The boy standing behind the empty chair starts the game by winking at one of the girls, who must immediately try to leave her chair and dash to the empty one. The boy standing behind her must try to stop her from going by tapping her on the shoulder. If he does this quickly enough she must remain where she is. If she succeeds in getting away, the boy who failed to keep her must then wink at some other girl in order to fill the chair in front of him. Whichever boy is doing the winking must use guile and cunning to obtain surprise. For instance, his wink can be almost imperceptible (except to the girl who is looking for it) or he can gaze steadily towards one part of the circle for a few seconds, then quickly turn his head and wink at a girl on the other side.

After a while, the boys and girls change places.

Fizz-buzz

All the players sit in a circle. One starts counting by saying 'One'. The next says 'Two', the third says 'Three', the fourth 'Four', but the fifth one, instead of saying, 'Five', says 'Fizz'. The sixth player says 'Six', but the seventh says 'Buzz'.

So the counting goes on; when a number is a multiple of five or has the digit 5 in it, the word 'Fizz' must be used, and when it is a multiple of seven or has the digit 7 in it, then it must be substituted with the word, 'Buzz'. When a number is a multiple of both five and seven or has both digits in it, then 'Fizz-Buzz' must be called.

Thus the numbers from eleven to twenty would be called: Eleven, twelve, thirteen, buzz, fizz, sixteen, buzz, eighteen, nineteen, fizz.

Reading in the train

1 They must all be rearranged identically; inserting some upside down adds to the fun.

2 The first one to hand in their newspaper with this done is the winner.

3 To begin this competition, you need a number of newspapers (one for each contestant); it is preferable that they should all be the same paper.

4 When you have muddled the pages, make a line of chairs as close together as possible, and ask the competitors to sit on them.

5 Having got the papers, rearrange the page order in them.

6 When everyone is sitting down, give the competitors the disarranged newspapers and tell them to put all the pages in the correct order as quickly as possible.

Name ______________________________ Date ______________

Party games

Answer these questions in sentences.

1 In the game 'Winking', how does the boy standing behind the chair stop the girl in front of him from escaping?

____

2 What word in the first passage means 'barely noticeable'?

____

3 What does the writer mean by 'guile and cunning'?

____

4 The instructions for playing 'Reading in the train' are in the wrong order. Write them out correctly. Use the back of this sheet if you need to.

a) ______________________________

b) ______________________________

c) ______________________________

d) ______________________________

e) ______________________________

f) ______________________________

5 Read again the instructions for playing 'Fizz-buzz'. What do you think a multiple of a number is?

____

6 Write out how you would call the numbers 21 to 30.

____

7 How could you change the game to make it easier?

____

8 Which game would you most enjoy playing? Give reasons.

____

Name ______________________________ Date ______________

The Ouse Valley cycle ride

ABOUT THE RIDE

There are two lengths of ride here, both worth doing. The area covered explores the delightful countryside of the Ouse Valley, passing through a number of picturesque villages. Both routes pass through Stevington, an historic village with much to see. The ride visits the watermill at Bromham which houses an interesting exhibition of mill artefacts.

1 This ride starts at the Bromham Mill car park. Leaving the car park, turn right and then right again into Bromham village. *Notice, on the left, the village school with an inscription round the eaves.*

2 At the junction, turn right to Oakley, *pausing at the bridge to see the river and the stone commemorating the flood water mark in 1823.*

3 Bear left and follow the road through the village and eventually to Pavenham. Here you must decide on the length of your ride. If it is to be a 10 mile trip turn left to Stevington. For the 16 mile trip, keep straight on to Felmersham.

4 For Felmersham, turn right at the T-junction and left at the next. *Allow a few minutes to look at the lofty church, medieval tithe barn, the bridge and the river. There is even a seat overlooking the river!*

5 Take the next left to Carlton, *a pleasant road which runs beside the Ouse Valley for 2 miles. On the way you will see the church with the tower at Odell and the two with spires at Chellington and Harrold. Along this road is Daisy Bank Picnic Site.*

6 At the junction after Carlton, take the right turn to Stevington. *Here there is much to see, including the 14th century stone cross where John Bunyan preached and the Holy Well. The lane to the left leads to the church which is well worth visiting.*
If you wish to visit the windmill, pick up the keys from the Royal George Inn and follow the Bromham road for a quarter of a mile where a footpath leads to the windmill. A wooden post mill built 1765–70, it was restored in 1951 and has an interesting interior ***Please return the keys****.*

7 Continue to Bromham turning left at the main road to arrive at Bromham Mill. *Bromham water mill was built in 1695 and is open from April to October, Wednesdays to Sundays. The interior contains the water wheels, millstones and agricultural tools as well as an art gallery and tea room and a nature study room.*

DISTANCE; 10 or 16 miles
RIDE: Easy
PUBS: The Rising Sun, Felmersham, Six Ringers, Felmersham, The Royal Oak, Felmersham
TEAS & SNACKS: Bromham Mill, when open

Name ______________________ Date ____________

The Ouse Valley cycle ride

Read carefully the instructions for the cycle route and then answer the questions.

1 There are two lengths of ride. How much further is the longer route?

____

2 How many churches are you able to see along the route?

____

3 The school has an 'inscription round the eaves'. What are the eaves? What do you think the inscription could be?

____

4 Why do you think the writer tells the reader that there is a seat overlooking the river at Felmersham? What is he suggesting?

____

5 What are the two types of mill mentioned? Which is the older of the two?

____

6 Why do you think part of the information is written in italic script?

____

7 Using the information given, label the route map below with the names of the villages.

____

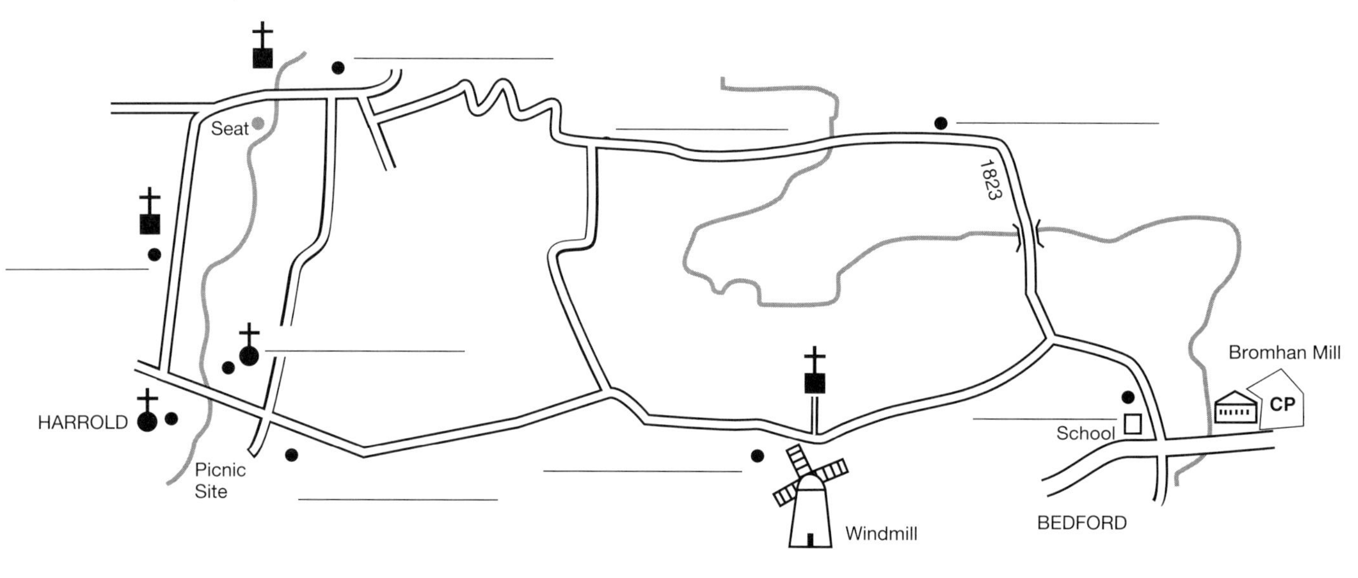

Name ______________________________ Date ______________

Flags

Flags began as markers to identify armies and leaders, such as kings, queens and generals. Before cloth flags were invented, these markers took the form of fixed objects on poles.

The Romans were the first to have a system of markers known as *standards* to identify their army. The standard would be an object, such as an eagle, fixed on top of a pole decorated with badges. The standard was carried by a soldier called a standard bearer.

Modern flags began around the time of the Crusades. King Richard the Lionheart of England (1189–99) used the symbol of three lions on his flag and wore it on his clothing and equipment. The symbol is still used today as the British Royal Standard – the official flag of the king or queen.

Flags are usually made from cloth. At one side is the *sleeve* and this is used to attach the flag to the *flagstaff*. A *hoist rope* which is sewn in the sleeve is attached to a long rope called a *halyard* and this is used to raise the flag. Each flag has a front called the *obverse* and a back called the *reverse*. The obverse is the side you see when the pole or flagstaff is on the left.

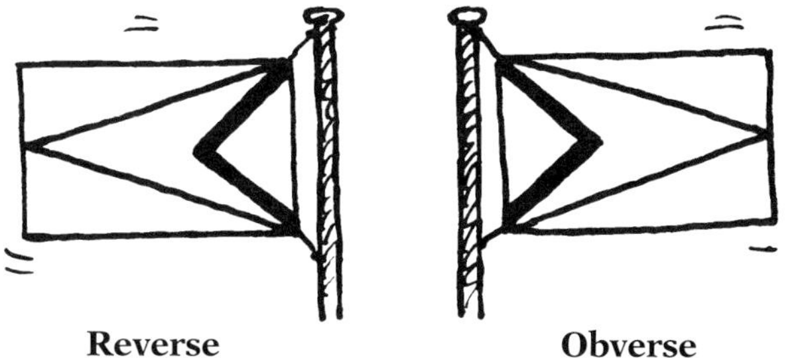

Every nation in the world has its own flag and many other groups and organisations have flags to represent them too. The flags of the world change frequently – new flags are invented as new countries are born or as their situation changes.

The following descriptions are of some flags representing African countries. The date tells when the flag was first used.

Algeria
1954

The flag is half green and half white, the green section is to the left. A large red crescent and 5-pointed star sit in the middle of the flag. The star lies within the crescent shape.

Central African Republic 1958

The flag is divided into four horizontal sections coloured from the top, blue, white, green and yellow. A broad red band runs vertically down the centre. In the top left corner of the blue section is a yellow 5-pointed star.

Niger
1959

This flag is divided into three horizontal sections coloured from the top, orange, white and green. In the centre of the white section is an orange circle.

Benin
1990

The flag has a vertical section coloured green. This covers about one-quarter of the flag. The remaining area is divided horizontally in half. The top part is yellow and the bottom is red.

Name ______________________ Date ______________

Flags

Read the information on flags and then answer the following questions.

1 Using the information given, draw and colour the African flags below. Make them as accurate as possible.

Niger	Benin	Algeria	Central African Republic

2 Write the ages of the flags in order, starting with the oldest.

a) __________ b) __________ c) __________ d) __________

3 What is the most common colour used in these flags?

____

4 What was the original purpose of markers or flags?

____

5 Explain in your own words where the term 'standard bearer' comes from.

____

6 Why do you think Richard used the symbol of lions to represent him on his flag?

____

7 On the back of this sheet, draw as carefully as you can a diagram of a flag flying from its pole and showing its obverse side. Make your own design on the flag and then label the following:

a) the flag b) the sleeve c) the hoist rope d) the halyard e) the flagstaff

Name ______________________ Date ______________

Diagnostic assessment – Factual/media

TEXAS TWISTER

TINY town is flattened as 200mph tornado flings trees, telegraph poles and lorries high into the air

It came with a greater speed than an express train. In just three minutes the 200mph tornado had engulfed a town, destroying everything in its path. Residents of Jarrell were sucked up like matchstick figures and buildings ripped apart as the roaring twister hurled down hailstones the size of cricket balls.

One 16-wheel lorry was lifted and dumped upside down 50 metres away.

Computer store owner, Mike Richardson, said: "The funnel was poking out of the sky and then the dirt on the ground began to spin. Then the top and bottom joined and the tornado started to move through the town."

CLOUD OF DANGER

A tornado is a dark funnel-shaped cloud containing violently twisting air which spirals down to earth. The funnel rotates as it rises and falls. Tornadoes are difficult to predict but are short-lived and violent.

1 Name the American town flattened by the tornado. Which state it is in?

____

2 How large were the hailstones? ______________________

3 At what speed was the tornado travelling? ______________________

Set A pages 42 - 45

4 Underline the word that does not describe a tornado.

violent destructive predictable speedy short-lived

5 What was the second stage of the tornado that Mike Richardson saw?

____

6 Which words mean the same as: goes round like a wheel?

____

Set B pages 46 - 49

7 Why do you think a tornado is often described as a 'twister'?

____

8 Why does the writer say 'like matchstick figures'?

____

9 How can people protect themselves from a tornado?

____

Set C pages 50 - 53

Name ______________________ Date ____________

THE SOLAR SYSTEM

THE SUN

The Sun is a huge ball of burning hot gases. It is about 150 million kilometres from the Earth. Without the Sun's light and warmth, the world would be a dead world. Planets near the Sun are very hot and those far away are very cold.

THE SUN'S FAMILY

The Sun's family is called the Solar System. As well as the Earth, eight other planets orbit the Sun. They are satellites of the Sun.

THE PLANETS

MERCURY

Mercury is the closest planet to the Sun. It has no atmosphere and nothing can survive on it.

VENUS

Venus is the closest planet to Earth and is about the same size but it would be impossible for us to live on Venus because it is very hot and clouds of deadly acid swirl round it. Venus can be seen in the night sky with the naked eye. It shines like a bright star.

EARTH

The Earth is the only planet on which we know there is life. It is different from all the other planets because conditions are just right for life to flourish. It is neither too hot nor too cold. It has water and it has an atmosphere which contains oxygen for breathing. It takes one year for Earth to orbit the Sun.

PLUTO

Pluto is the smallest planet and is about the size of the Earth. It is also the furthest away from the Sun. It takes nearly 250 years for Pluto to orbit the Sun!

MARS

Mars is the fourth planet from the Sun and is known as the Red Planet because chemicals in the soil give it a reddish-orange tinge. It is the only planet on which spacecraft from Earth have landed.

JUPITER, SATURN, URANUS AND NEPTUNE

These planets are all much larger than the Earth. In fact Jupiter is so big it could swallow 1,300 Earths! Saturn is easily recognisable by the many rings around it. All these planets are made up of gases rather than rock.

Name ______________________ Date ____________

The solar system

Using the information given, label the remaining planets.

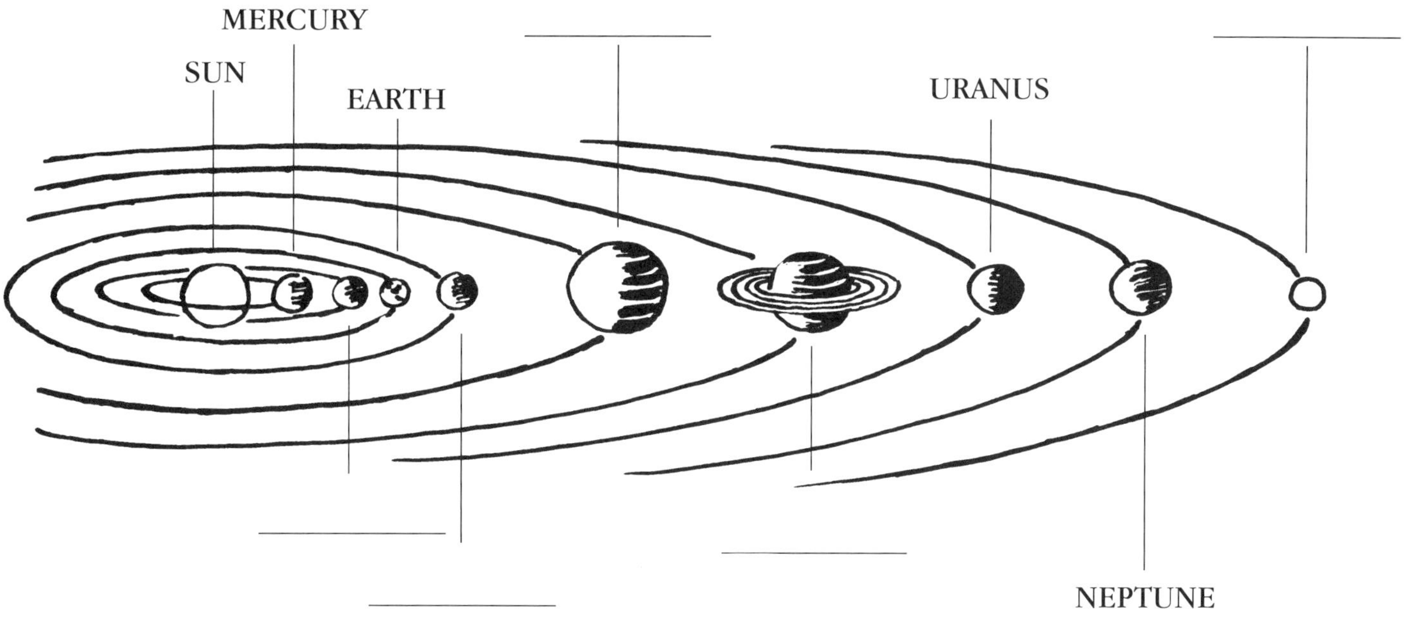

Answer these questions in sentences.

1 How many planets are there in our solar system?

____

2 Why is Mars called the Red Planet?

____

3 Does the Earth move round the Sun or the Sun move round the Earth?

____

4 Could a spacecraft land on Jupiter? Give reasons for your answer.

____

5 Explain in your own words why Earth is the only planet with living things.

____

6 Name three planets that are made from rock.

____

7 Why do you think the solar system is called the Sun's family?

____

Name ______________________ Date ____________

WINDOW ON A WORLD WHERE TIME STANDS STILL

MRS. SMITH was old-fashioned and enjoyed a simple life.

For most of her 103 years, she lived without the mod-cons most people take for granted, and her cottage became a time capsule of life in a bygone age. Some parts of the house are untouched since it was built nearly 200 years ago. Now, two years after her death and with the help of a £65,000 lottery grant, 'Mrs. Smith's Cottage' is to open as a museum.

The old lady was so popular that she would receive a continuous stream of visitors to drink tea and listen to her wonderful stories by the 19th century black-leaded range. It was after she died that locals realised what a treasure she had left and launched a campaign to save it. The cottage has just four rooms on two floors and so little has been done to the building that the two upstairs rooms remain completely separate, with no access to each other. Every night the widow would retire to bed by way of a pull-down ladder, thought to date back to 1800. She said it was easier than a staircase.

Both her bedroom and the spare have little furniture and have only one tiny window each. All her clothes were kept in antique linen chests and her washing jug still stands on the dressing table.

The oak-beamed sitting room is lined with dusty books and faded photographs and is furnished with two armchairs and a bookcase.

With no central heating or running hot water, Mrs. Smith cooked on the range which dates back to 1850. It may be a museum piece but Mrs. Smith cooked joints and milk puddings on it until her final days. Although connected to the mains, the cottage has hardly any electrical appliances. There is no fridge, microwave, washing machine or telephone. She washed clothes and dishes in the tiny scullery. She had one tap but insisted on scooping her water from the well in the garden. For most of her life she also used an outside toilet.

She spent nearly all her adult years living alone. She married in 1956 but her husband died just five years later.

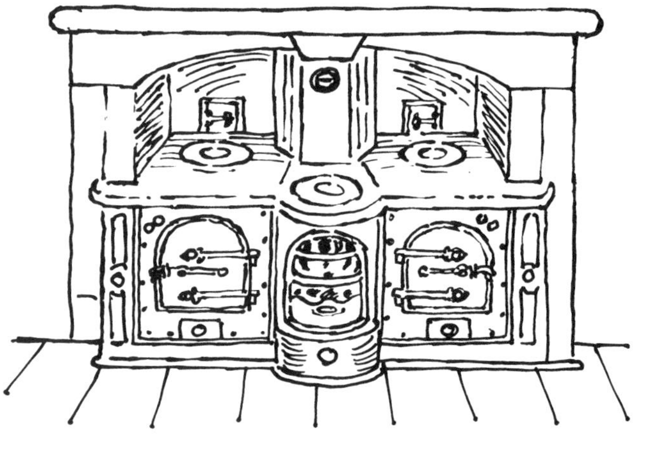

Name ______________________ Date ____________

Mrs. Smith's cottage

Which of the following statements are true? Write true or false beside each statement.

Mrs. Smith liked to keep up with modern technology. ________

Parts of Mrs. Smith's cottage had not changed for nearly 200 years. ________

Mrs. Smith never married and had always lived alone. ________

The two bedrooms led into each other. ________

Mrs. Smith told stories to her visitors while they drank tea. ________

Local people helped raise money to make the cottage a museum. ________

Mrs. Smith had no electricity or running water in her cottage. ________

Answer the following in sentences.

1 Where did Mrs. Smith get her water from?

____

2 How did Mrs. Smith do her cooking?

____

3 Mrs. Smith's cottage only had four rooms – two upstairs and two downstairs. Name the two downstairs rooms.

____

4 How did Mrs. Smith get to her bedroom? Why did she choose to do this?

____

5 Which words tell us that Mrs. Smith had a lot of visitors?

____

6 Do you think Mrs. Smith had a hard life? Give reasons for your answer.

____

Name ______________________ Date ____________

Happy Homes

The Chaffinch

Finches

The Finches, High Street, Walkern
(Stevenage Station 10 minutes drive)
fast service to London

4 Bedroom Detached Homes
close to the River Beane and open farmland

Finches Farm

A country development of 18 homes set on a site which runs down to the River Beane and overlooks open farmland.

With six different house types and a variety of materials and finishes, each property will have an individual feel. There are 9 four-bedroom detached houses, 5 five-bedroom detached houses, all with double garages and 4 two-bedroom bungalows.

The specification includes gas-fired central heating and double glazed sealed units. For those buying early, there are many opportunities to further personalise your new home with a choice of kitchen finishes and a chance to select bathroom suite colours and styles.

Those who know Walkern enjoy this lively village with its own school, shop, 3 popular hostelries and other businesses. There are local football and cricket teams that help to provide plenty of activity.

The Chaffinch

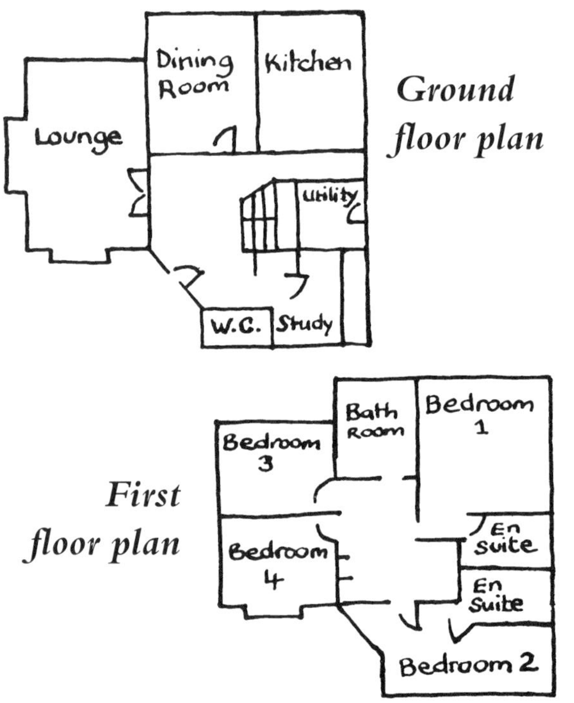

Plot 2 – The Chaffinch
4 bed detached house
£225,000

Name ______________________ Date ____________

Happy homes

Read the advertisement and answer the following questions.

1 Underline the correct answer.

The price of the Chaffinch is a) £200,000 b) £225,000 c) £250,000 d) £275,000

The houses are heated by a) solid fuel b) oil-fired central heating c) gas d) electricity

The new homes overlook a) Stevenage station b) open farmland c) the cricket ground d) a bird sanctuary

2 The house shown is called the Chaffinch. Why do you think the builders chose this name?

____

3 How is the buyer able to make their house feel more individual?

____

4 Are we told that the two bedroom homes have garages?

____

5 What is a) a detached house? b) a bungalow?

a) ____________ b) ____________

6 Which of the homes at Finches Farm would be most suitable for:
a) a retired couple? b) a family of six? Give your reasons.

a) ______________________

b) ______________________

7 The building company is called Happy Homes. Do you think this is a good name for house builders? Give your reasons.

____

____

Name ______________________ Date ____________

Martial arts

Judo

The aim of judo, which means 'the soft way', is not to hurt your opponent but to show skill in carrying out the different judo throws. The judo costume of jacket, trousers and belt is called the *judogi*. The jacket has to be very tough because of all the tugging that goes on during a bout. Competitors go barefoot on the mat but have to cover their feet as soon as they leave it. The colour of the belt worn by judo competitors shows how good they are. The grades range from white to yellow, orange, green, blue and brown. Then comes the famous black belt.

Sumo wrestling

In Japan, top sumo wrestlers are treated like superstars. In a fight, wrestlers use their enormous bulk to try to push each other right out of the combat circle. Hawaiian wrestler, Konishiki, known as the Dump Truck, weighs 225 kilograms. It would take nine small girls to equal his weight. The wrestlers eat huge amounts of a high protein stew called *chanko-nabe*.

Karate

Contestants in karate hit out with their hands, arms and feet to score points. Contests normally last for two minutes and are controlled by a referee and four judges. Actual physical contact is not required to score points – as with judo, it is superior technique that counts.

Fencing

Fencing is a combat sport using swords. The three types of sword are the *foil*, the *epee* and the *sabre*. Fencing swords do not have cutting blades and the tip is formed into a blunt button to prevent injuries. Only the tip of the sword can be used to score points. Contestants still wear strong protective clothing to stop them from coming to any harm.

Kite fighting

One combat sport that is unlikely to hurt anybody is kite fighting. Flyers use their kites to move the special glass coated line backwards and forwards over their opponent's line. This cuts the line and sends the enemy kite spiraling out of control.

Name ______________________ Date ____________

Martial arts

Read the information carefully and then answer the questions in sentences.

1 a) What does the word *judo* mean?

b) What is meant by a *combat* sport?

2 If you gained a black belt in judo, what would this mean?

3 Which sporting contest lasts for two minutes only?

4 Give two ways in which fencing swords are made safe.

5 What 'weapon' does a sumo wrestler use to defeat his opponent?

6 What is a) judogi? b) chanko-nabe?

a) ______________ b) ______________

7 Which sport mentioned is least likely to harm anyone? Why do you think this is true?

8 In what way are we told that karate is like judo?

9 Which of the sports mentioned would you most like to learn? Give reasons for your answer.

Continue on the back of this sheet.

Name ______________________________ Date ______________

How our ears work

If you have ever played a drum, you will know what happens when you hit it. The surface of the drum trembles, or vibrates. The sound the drum makes is caused by the vibration. All sounds are sets of vibrations. They travel through the air as sound waves.

Our ears are the parts of our body that receive sound. They turn the sound into messages and pass them to the brain.

The ear is made up of three main parts. These are the outer ear, the middle ear and the inner ear. The outer ear is the part we can see. This is shaped to pick up as much sound as possible.

The sound travels down a short passage which leads to the eardrum. The sound hits the eardrum and makes it vibrate. The sound vibrations are passed from the eardrum along two small bones called the hammer and anvil. They are then passed along a group of tiny bones called the stirrup. These bones are part of the middle ear.

The bones of the middle ear send the sound waves through to the inner ear. Part of this is the cochlea, which is curled in shape. Nerves in the cochlea turn the sound waves into messages which are sent to the brain.

Keeping our balance

What happens when you spin round and round very fast? Do you feel dizzy when you stop? Can you walk straight? You may even fall over. When this happens, your sense of balance is upset. After a short while it returns to normal.

The brain learns about the body's balance from a group of tubes in the inner ear. These are the semi-circular canals. Inside the canals are tiny hairs which respond to every movement you make. They pass signals on to the brain. The brain can then correct your movements if it needs to. When you stop spinning round, the fluid in the canals carries on moving. This upsets your balance because the nerves still react to the moving fluid. The brain tries to make corrections, but these make you fall over.

Why do we need two ears?

We need both ears to work out where sounds are coming from. Try this and see. Turn on the radio. Cover your eyes, cover up one ear, and turn round a few times. Where is the radio?

Name ______________________ Date ____________

How our ears work

Read the information carefully and then answer the following questions.

1 From the information given in the first section, label the diagram below. One label has been done for you.

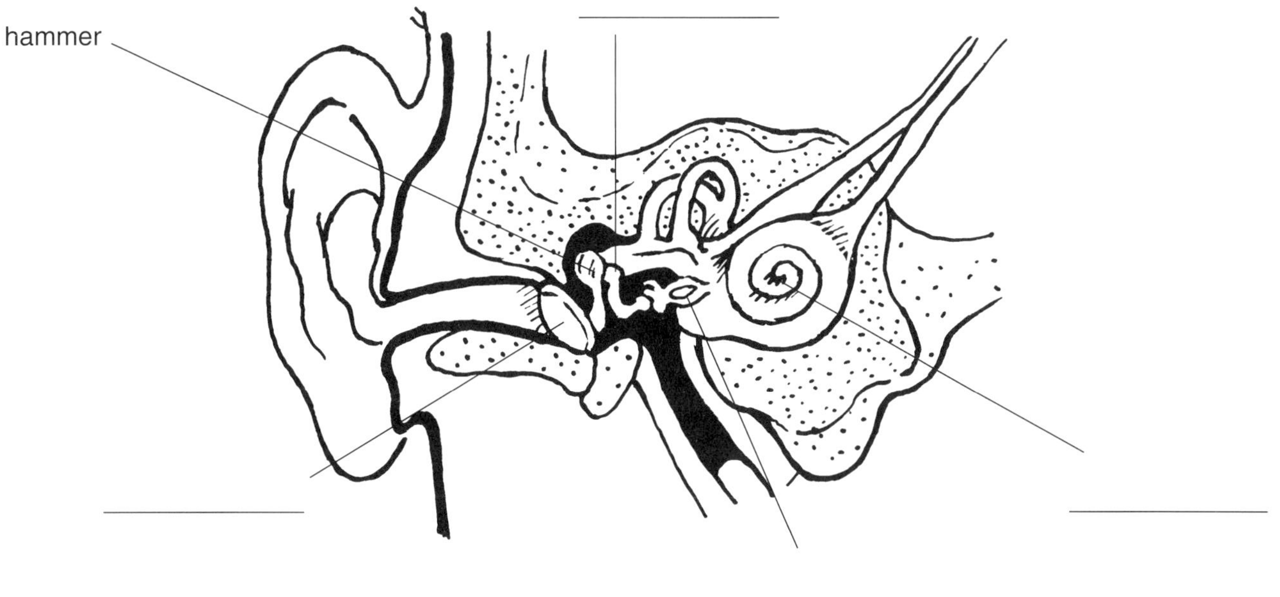

2 What does the word 'vibrate' mean?

3 What three things may happen if you spin round very fast?

4 What is the name of the group of tubes in the ear that controls our balance?

5 What is it that passes the movement signals on to the brain?

6 Explain in your own words what makes you fall over if you get dizzy.

7 What would happen if you only had one ear?

8 What are the two important jobs that the ear has to do?

Name ______________________ Date ____________

Reindeer

If you are going off in search of reindeer, don't try to identify one by its red nose. Reindeer are actually the least likely of any deer to get red noses in cold weather – this is because they are completely covered in warm fur. This thick fur protects them from the cold climates of Scandinavia and Russia where they mostly live. The fur is particularly dense underneath with thick, hollow outer hairs which work together to keep the reindeer warm. This fur is also very buoyant and acts like a life jacket whenever the reindeer goes in water.

OFF COLOUR

Reindeer coats come in a variety of colours – they can be grey, off white, beige or brown. Although reindeer were once wild and roamed in herds, many are now semi-domesticated and kept by people like the Lapps in northern Sweden who farm them for their milk, meat and pelts.

Wild and most semi-domesticated reindeer roam mountains and forests feeding on soft plants. Leaves, herbs, roots of swamp plants, fungi and especially tree and ground lichens are all on the menu. Lichens are very good for reindeer as they are high in carbohydrates which provide lots of energy.

NEW ADDITIONS

Reindeer calves are born in the spring and are quite strong. Within one hour of birth they can stand up. Until six months old the calf will feed from its mother's rich milk and stay quite close by her side. After six months it will take its place with the rest of the herd. Female reindeer live about ten years in the wild, but males live a shorter six to eight years.

HIGHLAND DEER

In Scotland there is a large domestic herd. These reindeer were brought over from Sweden between 1952 and 1961 and are now about 70-strong.

WINTER WHITES

Winter is very difficult for wild reindeer – they have to dig through thick snow and ice to find food. Although they can dig down through 120cm of snow with their large hooves, this becomes just about impossible when the snow thaws and then freezes again. During winter, reindeer tend to lose weight and also move territory – migrate – in search of food. Some migrations can involve travelling over 1000km a year.

Reindeer mate in the autumn between September and October. This period is described as the rut. Male reindeer (stags) will fight each other for the female (cow). Sometimes these fights are very violent and can end in injury or even the death of a stag. After the rut, the stags shed their antlers which means they have no antlers at all during the winter. The cows, however, keep theirs until just a couple of days after their calves are born.

REINDEER ENEMIES

The main natural enemy of the reindeer is the wolf. Wolves tend to attack and eat sick or weak animals. Newborn calves may be attacked and eaten by red foxes, Arctic foxes, crows and bears. Reindeer also have other, smaller enemies. Biting insects like mosquitoes, black flies and gnats attack them in the summer months and reindeer spend a lot of time moving about to try and shake them off. Humans also cause the reindeer problems – pollution, low flying aircraft, snowmobiles, hikers, campers and skiers can all stress the reindeer or ruin their environment.

Name ______________________ Date ____________

Reindeer

Read the information carefully and then answer the following questions.

1 Which section gives information about a) reindeer young b) reindeer eating habits

a) ______________________ b) ______________________

2 Explain how reindeer stay afloat in water.

____

3 Which word in the 'Winter Whites' section means to move to another area?

____

4 What is the 'rut'?

____

5 'Although all reindeer were once wild and roamed in herds, many are now semi-domesticated.' What does semi-domesticated mean?

____

6 Name three foods mentioned in the passage which are eaten by the reindeer. Which type of food gives the reindeer high energy?

____

7 What is the correct name for a) a male reindeer? b) a female reindeer? c) a young reindeer?

a) ____________ b) ____________ c) ____________

8 Where do reindeer mostly live? Can you still see them in Britain?

____

9 'Pollution, low flying aircraft, snowmobiles, hikers, campers and skiers can all stress the reindeer or ruin their *environment*.' What do you think this means?

____

____

Name ______________________ Date ____________

Diagnostic assessment

Once upon a time a lion was snoozing in the sun. A tiny mouse woke him by running across his paw. The lion was just about to squash the mouse when the mouse spoke.

"Please don't hurt me, mighty lion. If you help me by letting me go, I may be able to help you one day."

"You!" roared the lion, "help me? As if you, a little nothing, could possibly help me, the king of all beasts! Yes, I will let you go. You deserve it for your impudence."

The lion roared again as the mouse scampered away.

Several days later, she heard the lion's thunderous roar again. To her amazement she found her lion trapped in an enormous net, put down by hunters. The more the lion struggled and roared, the more entangled he became. He was becoming wilder with anger and frustration.

"I can help you," said the mouse.

"You!" roared the lion. "You won't be able to help me."

"Stay still," she ordered as she began to gnaw and nibble at the rope. Soon she had made a hole big enough to free the lion. "Thank you, mouse," he said. "I shall never again judge someone by what they look like. You are much stronger and more useful than you look."

"It's a pleasure," she said as she scampered off. "One good turn deserves another."

1 Why did the lion wake up from his sleep?

____

2 How did the lion become trapped?

____

3 Explain how the mouse freed the lion.

____

Set A
pages 55 - 58

4 How did the mouse persuade the lion not to harm her?

____

5 Which words in the passage mean the same as:

a) cheekiness ____________ b) very noisy ____________

6 Think of a suitable word to describe:

a) the lion ____________ b) the mouse ____________

Set B
pages 59 - 62

7 "One good turn deserves another." What does this mean?

____

8 What opinion did the lion have of the mouse when he first met her? How did this change?

____

9 This story is a fable. A fable has a moral; it teaches us a lesson about behaviour. Can you find any moral to this story?

____

Set C
pages 63 - 64

Name ______________________________ Date ____________

Pablo Picasso

Not very long ago, lived a very famous painter called Picasso. Picasso painted pictures, lots of pictures, during his lifetime. Some people liked his pictures and said, “Picasso is one of the greatest painters who ever lived. Picasso’s paintings are different, original, unique. Picasso’s paintings are wonderful.” Other people looked at Picasso’s paintings, many of which were more like patterns than pictures, and they said, “What rubbish! He can’t paint for toffee. Look at the paintings, they don’t even look like what they are supposed to be. Any fool can paint pictures like that!”

But those people were wrong. For what they didn’t know was that before Picasso began to paint his pictures-like-patterns, he learned how to paint ‘properly’. He learned about paint and canvasses and brushes. He learned about light and shade, and how to paint so that the things he painted looked real enough to touch. In the beginning, when he first began to paint, he painted pictures that looked as real as photographs. Then he began to feel dissatisfied; he wanted to paint pictures that were different, pictures that were his, pictures that people would look at and say, “Picasso painted that”, without even looking at his name in the corner. So Picasso began to experiment with colours and shapes, and he began to paint his pattern-pictures. He developed his own way of painting, but only after he had learned to paint ‘properly’.

Pablo Picasso was born in 1881 and died in 1973. He was Spanish by birth but lived and worked in France. He was one of the most influential artists of the 20th century, famous as a painter and a sculptor. In total, he created more than 20,000 works of art.

These pictures are like Picasso’s later style.

Name ______________________ Date ____________

Pablo Picasso

Read the information carefully and then answer the following questions.

1 What nationality was Picasso?

____

2 How long ago did Picasso die? How old was he?

____

3 How does the author describe Picasso's early pictures?
Complete the sentence:

'They' looked as real as ______________________

4 How were Picasso's later pictures described?

____

5 What are the meanings of the words 'original' and 'unique' which were used to describe Picasso's paintings?

____

6 Complete the sentence by writing suitable words in the spaces.

Some people thought Picasso's paintings were ____________ , others thought they were ____________ .

7 What is a sculptor?

____

8 Why did Picasso begin to feel 'dissatisfied' with his work?

____

9 What do you think is meant by the sentence: 'He was one of the most influential artists of the 20th century'?

____

Name ______________________________ Date ______________

How to make a kaleidoscope

1 On the plain side of the mirror board, mark off every 5cm along one edge. Do the same on the opposite side and join the marks.

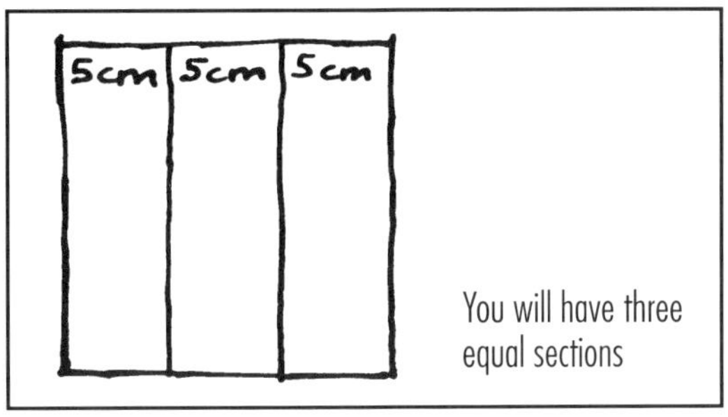

What you need:
15cm square mirror board
1 sheet wrapping paper
tracing paper
felt pens
sticky tape and glue
pencil, scissors and a ruler

2 Score along the lines using a ruler and the tip of the scissors.
DO NOT CUT RIGHT THROUGH THE CARD

3 Fold the board along the lines so the mirror is inside and stick the edges together with tape.

4 Stand the tube on tracing paper and trace round the end. Do the same with the wrapping paper.

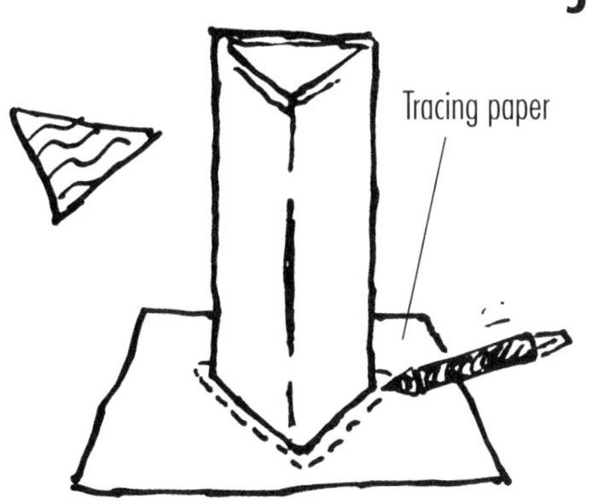

5 Cut out the triangles of paper. Stick the triangle of tracing paper over one end.

6 Colour pieces of tracing paper with felt pens. Cut them into bits and drop them into the tube.

7 Stick the triangle of wrapping paper over the other end of the tube and make a hole in the middle with the pencil.

8 Cut out a piece of wrapping paper 17cm long and 15cm wide. Lay the tube on the paper and glue the paper neatly round the tube.

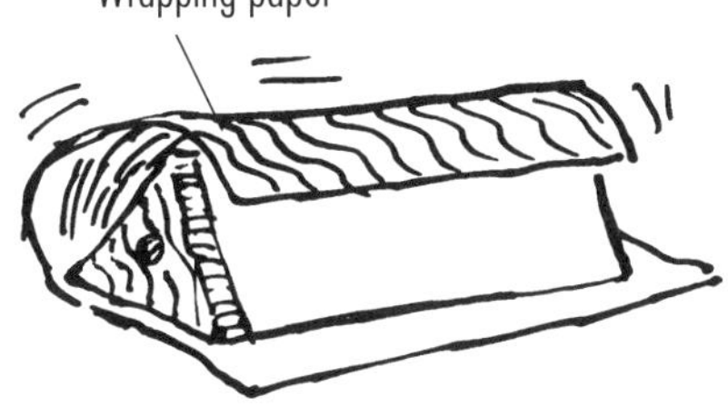

9 Hold the tube up to the light and look through the hole. You will see patterns through your kaleidoscope. Shake the kaleidoscope and see the patterns change.

Name ______________________ Date ____________

How to make a kaleidoscope

Read the instructions carefully and then answer the following questions.

1 Which two pieces of equipment do you need to 'score' card?

____

2 How are we told to make the hole in the wrapping paper?

____

3 What will you see when you look through the kaleidoscope?

____

4 What do you think 'score' means? What is the purpose of scoring card?

____

5 Why is it necessary to put tracing paper over one end of the tube? Why couldn't you put wrapping paper over both ends?

____

6 Underline the correct answer.

(i) You need mirror board because: a) it is prettier than plain card b) it reflects the coloured shapes c) it is easier to fold

(ii) The small coloured pieces of tracing paper: a) are used for decoration b) stop the light reflecting c) make the changing pattern

7 Why do you think the list of equipment is given at the beginning?

____

8 Do you think it would be easy to make this kaleidoscope? Give reasons for your answer.

____

Name ______________________ Date ____________

COOPERS OPEN FARM

CROWBRIDGE RD
OXTHORPE
TEL 01212 341180

RARE BREEDS

ABOUT THE FARM

Coopers Farm is a family farm just outside Oxthorpe. We provide an entertaining and educational day out for all the family.

The farm is 400 hectares (approx 1000 acres) and encompasses both arable and livestock farming.

There is a wide range of animals including sheep, pigs, cows, horses, hens, ducks, turkeys and goats. The animals are housed in paddocks and farm buildings where they can easily be seen and touched.

There are also some rare breeds including Oxford and Sandy pigs, Highland cows and Castle Morrit sheep.

Crops grown include wheat, barley and Brussels sprouts.

The farmer is never far away and is always pleased to meet children and answer questions.

We can provide learning aids, such as measuring equipment, a rain gauge, a wind meter and a weathervane. There are also opportunities for soil sampling/profiling, crop measurement etc.

ADMISSION DETAILS

Opening hours:
9.00a.m - 5.30p.m. Tues - Sun
Closed on Mondays except Bank Holidays and school holidays.

Entrance:
£3.50 adults £1.75 children
Group discounts (over 10 persons)
£2.50 adults £1.25 children.

WHAT IS THERE TO DO?

- This is a working farm so there are often seasonal activities, such as ploughing and combine harvesting that can be witnessed at first hand.
- Make friends with the small animals in Pets Corner. Most of them can be safely handled and fed by hand.
- Stroll around the lake and observe nature and wildlife.
- See newborn piglets and calves throughout the year.
- See the cows being milked.
- Feed the newborn lambs in Spring.
- Play on our Adventure Playground or picnic in Buttercup Meadow.
- Enjoy a snack or a hot meal in our tea rooms.

New this year:-

- Hedgerow walk.
- Extra undercover facilities in case of inclement weather.

HOW TO FIND US

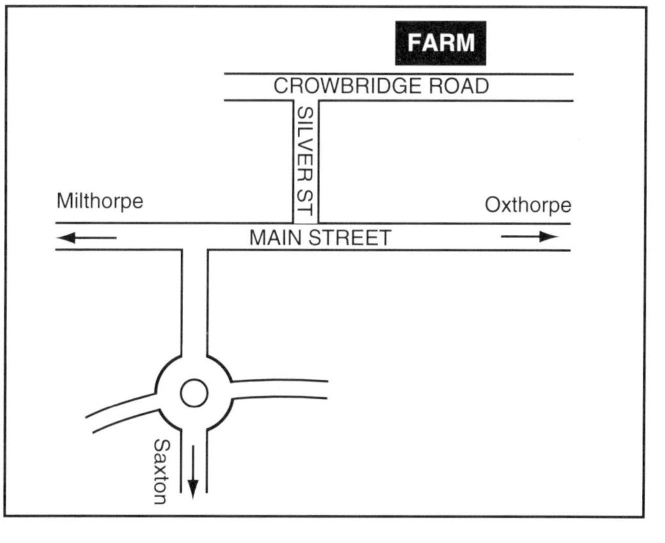

Name ____________________ Date ____________

Coopers Open Farm

Answer these questions in sentences.

1 a) Where would you find Coopers Farm?
b) Why do you think it is called an open farm?

a) ____________________

b) ____________________

2 It is both an arable and livestock farm. What do you think an arable farm is?

____

3 Which crop mentioned is not a grain crop?

____

4 Explain in your own words a) rare breeds b) inclement weather.

a) ____________________

b) ____________________

5 How much is the group discount for a) an adult? b) a child?

a) ____________________

b) ____________________

6 How would you reach Coopers Farm if you were travelling from Saxton?

____

____

7 If you were the farm's owner, what additional attractions would you provide?

____

____

8 Would the farm be suitable for a school visit? Give reasons for your answer.

____

____

Name ______________________ Date ______________

Trapped!

Smiler was on the run from the police and had taken shelter in the loft of a hay barn. The previous night he had left the door to the barn open while he took out his rubbish and washed in the nearby river. On his return, he went to bed without realising that a visitor had crept into the barn!

The brightening crack of light under the barn door woke Yarra. She rolled over and sat up on her haunches. She tightened the muscles of her long forelegs to ease the night's laziness from them. She sat, sphinx-fashion in the gloom like an ancient Egyptian cat goddess, her liquid amber eyes watching the light under the door. Although the door was closed, and had not been the previous night, it did not seem strange to her. The door of her hut at Longleat was always closed during the night and the warden opened it early in the morning. She sat waiting for the sound of his feet outside. Sometimes he was early and sometimes late.

Half an hour passed and the warden did not come. Yarra rose to her feet, walked to the door and sniffed at it. Then she turned back along the far wall. Her restlessness was coming back fast. She wanted to be outside, where the world was full of sounds, blackbirds and sparrows calling, the beat of a car's engine passing down the narrow road and the low, mocking caws of rooks moving from their night roosts to forage on the iron-hard field furrows.

Annoyed now, she raised herself on her hind feet and scraped against the shut door, rattling and banging it impatiently.

The scraping, rattling and banging from down below eventually woke Smiler. He lay on his hay bed, still a little muzzy with sleep, listening to it. It took him a minute or two to remember where he was. When he did, he jumped quickly to his feet and stood above the trap door. Somebody was down below! With the thought his heart began to thump with alarm. He knelt down and cautiously lifted the lid of the loft trap an inch and peered through. His eyes, dazed from the sunlight which was streaming in through the loft window, could make out nothing in the gloom below. Then, as his eyes slowly adjusted themselves, he saw the movement at the barn door. For a moment or two he watched, his mouth open in amazement. Then – with a swift, panic reaction – he slammed the trapdoor and shot across the holding bolt which was fastened to the top of it. He dropped back to a sitting position on the hay, clapped a hand to his forehead, and said out loud,"Blimey O' Reilly!"

Name ______________________________ Date ______________

Trapped!

Read the passage carefully and answer the following questions in sentences.

1 What woke Smiler from his sleep?

____

2 Why was Smiler alarmed when he thought someone was in the barn?

____

3 How did Yarra get into the barn?

____

4 What sort of animal do you think Yarra is? Give your evidence.

____

____

5 Why was Yarra not concerned when she first found the door closed?

____

6 Why couldn't Smiler see anything through the trapdoor at first?

____

7 Why do you think he was so amazed when he realised what was in the barn below?

____

8 What do you think is meant by 'forage on the iron-hard field furrows'?

____

9 What do you think Smiler will do next?

____

____

Name ______________________________ Date ______________

The woodland haiku

A Slinks to the wood's edge
and – with one paw raised –
surveys the open meadows.

B Blind panic sets in
and they're off, like dodgem
cars gone out of control.

C *Blip* on his radar
sends him whooshing
through the dark, homing
in on rats, mice.

D Moving smooth as smoke
she starts at an air tremor.
Is gone like a ghost.

E They float high above,
black as scraps of charred
paper drifting from a fire.

F Killer submarine
he lurks deep in the woodland's
green-skinned pond. Lurks...strikes

G Clumsy, twig snapping,
they see nothing but trees, trees
The creatures hide...watch...

Titles

Owl	Humans
Pike	Fox
Rabbits	Fallow Deer
Rooks	

Name ______________________________ Date ______________

The woodland haiku

Haiku is a form of Japanese poetry which consists of three lines and 17 syllables in the pattern of 5–7–5. Read carefully the seven *Haiku* verses.

1 Allocate the correct title from those listed below the poems, to each of the following letters.

A ______________________________

B ______________________________

C ______________________________

D ______________________________

E ______________________________

F ______________________________

G ______________________________

2 Which words can you find in the haiku that have similar meanings to the following?

a) having a general look at something ______________________

b) shaking or trembling movement ______________________

c) move in a stealthy way______________________

d) wait where you cannot be seen ______________________

e) blackened by burning ______________________

f) guiding to a target ______________________

3 Answer these questions in sentences.

i What do you think is meant by 'Blip on his radar'?

____

ii What do you think animal F is catching?

____

iii Why do you think the creatures 'hide' and 'watch' animal G?

____

iv Do you think 'The woodland haiku' is a suitable name?

____